MW01247524

ORGANIZE YOUR CLOSET

Kevin Wagonfoot

Copyright © 2024 Kevin Wagonfoot

All rights reserved

The characters and events portrayed in this book are fictitious. Any similarity to real persons, living or dead, is coincidental and not intended by the author.

ISBN: 9798325183522

No part of this book may be reproduced, or stored in a retrieval system, or transmitted in any form or by any means, electronic, mechanical, photocopying, recording, or otherwise, without express written permission of the publisher.

CONTENTS

INTRODUCTION

Simplicity is the ultimate sophistication

— LEONARDO DA VINCI

Like many, my closet was once a realm of disarray. Each morning was a challenge, sifting through piles of clothes, struggling to find something suitable to wear that wasn't part of my daily uniform. It wasn't just about the mess; it was about how this clutter made me feel—overwhelmed and disorganized in more ways than one.

Everything changed when I moved to a new apartment. This move was my catalyst for change, a perfect opportunity to break free from the clutter that had unwittingly become a significant part of my life. I was determined not to bring my old, disorganized habits into my new space. Inspired by this fresh start, I delved into researching the best ways to organize a closet and, more importantly, how to keep it organized.

What I discovered was transformative, and the methods I adopted turned my daily frustration into a harmonious routine. I learned not just how to arrange my clothes but how to maintain this order with ease, making my daily routine smoother and my mornings more enjoyable.

This is what my closet looked like!

In this book, I want to share with you all that I have learned and practiced successfully. Whether you're looking for a complete overhaul or just some tips to tweak your existing setup, my goal is to help you create a space that supports and enhances your lifestyle. Let's begin on this journey together, transforming cluttered closets into spaces of serenity and efficiency.

The Psychological Impact Of Organization

A tidy environment is more than just pleasing to the eye—it can significantly affect our mental and emotional well-being. Research has shown that clutter can overwhelm the brain, leading to increased stress and anxiety. In contrast, an organized space can promote a sense of calm and control, reducing tension and enhancing our ability to focus and process information. It's about lowering physical clutter and fostering a peaceful and efficient mental environment. This is why organization matters—it's a step towards a healthier, more balanced life.

Saving Time And Enhancing Productivity

One of the most immediate benefits of organizing your space, particularly your closet, is the time saved during daily routines. Imagine a morning where everything you need is at your fingertips, without the need to sift through piles of clothes or miscellaneous items. This streamlined process doesn't just save time—it enhances your productivity throughout the day. An organized start leads to a more structured and efficient daily routine, providing more time for personal and professional pursuits.

Economic Benefits Of Organization

Proper organization of your belongings extends their life and saves you money in the long run. Maintaining an orderly space reduces the likelihood of losing items, often leading to unnecessary replacements. Moreover, you're less likely to make impulsive buys or purchase duplicates with everything in its place. This mindful approach to consumption can significantly impact your financial health, making organization an economically wise choice.

Aesthetic Pleasures Of A Well-Organized Closet

Beyond functionality, there's undeniable aesthetic pleasure in a well-organized closet. This space can serve as a personal showroom where everything is displayed elegantly, making choosing what to wear daily a delightful experience rather than a frustrating chore. The beauty of a thoughtfully arranged closet is not just in its appearance but also in the ease and joy it brings to your daily routine.

Envisioning Your Ideal Closet

As we look into the practical aspects of closet organization, we encourage you to envision your ideal closet. What does it look like? How does it function? This vision will guide you in selecting the right tools and strategies to transform your current closet into one that looks great and enhances your lifestyle.

The journey to a well-organized closet is about sorting, decluttering, and creating a space that reflects and supports your lifestyle and values. As we proceed, remember that the goal is not perfection but functionality and personal satisfaction. Let's take this step towards a more organized and fulfilling life together.

I have a special gift for you. I've written a helpful companion book, "**Organize Your Cleaning**," I'd love to share a complimentary copy with you. *Learn how to easily clean anything in your house, and keep it that way in under 15 minutes a day!*

Just visit **KevinWagonfoot.com**, enter your email address, and the book is yours. Plus, by signing up, you'll receive my weekly newsletter covering various topics, from mental models and performance enhancements to practical tips for organizing your life.

GETTING
STARTED

CHAPTER 1: ASSESSING YOUR NEEDS

An organized life is a life that is easy to navigate

— ERNA SOLBERG

Welcome to the first step in transforming your closet: Assessing your needs. This chapter will help you understand what you have and need and how your closet can better serve your lifestyle. It's about making your closet not just a place to store clothes but a functional space that supports your daily life.

Conducting An Inventory

Begin by taking everything out of your closet. Yes, everything. This might seem daunting at first, but it's essential for seeing exactly what you own and how it fits into your life. Lay out all your clothing, accessories, and shoes. As you do this, you'll likely rediscover items you've forgotten about and see clearly what you use and don't.

Categorizing Your Items

Once all your items are visible, start categorizing them. Create categories like workwear, casual wear, special occasion outfits, and seasonal items. This will help you see what types of clothing you have most and what areas might be lacking or overly stocked. Understanding these categories will assist you in making decisions about what to keep and what might need updating.

Identifying Frequently Used Items

As you sort through your categories, pay special attention to the items you repeatedly reach for. These are your essentials, the backbone of your wardrobe. Noting these favorites is crucial because ensuring they are accessible and well-maintained will make your daily routine smoother.

Assessing Lifestyle Needs

Your closet should reflect your lifestyle. If you attend many formal events, your closet will look different from someone who wears a uniform to work every day. Take a moment to consider your weekly activities. Do you need quick access to gym clothes? Do you dress in layers for a commute? These lifestyle considerations will influence how you organize and prioritize the space in your closet.

Setting Achievable Goals

With a clear understanding of what you own and your lifestyle needs, set specific goals for your closet space. These goals range from simply wanting to reduce clutter to creating a dedicated area for each type of clothing. Goals should be realistic and measurable, such as "I want to reduce my wardrobe by 20%" or "I need to have all my work clothes in one easily accessible section."

Planning For Function And Accessibility

Think about how you use your closet daily. What works well? What frustrates you? You may need more hanging space or additional shelves for shoes. Assessing these functional needs will help you plan a closet that looks good and works well for your daily life.

Assessing your closet is not just about sorting through clothes—it's about reassessing your relationship with your wardrobe and how it fits into your life. This chapter sets the foundation for making informed decisions that will shape the next steps in organizing your space effectively. By understanding what you have and need, you can create a closet that enhances your daily routine and brings simplicity and joy into your day-to-day life.

CHAPTER 2: DECLUTTERING BASICS

Decluttering is infinitely more manageable when you think of it as deciding what to keep rather than deciding what to throw away

— FRANCINE JAY

Welcome to the essential phase of transforming your closet: decluttering. This chapter will guide you through a straightforward process for clearing out what you don't need and making room for items that enhance your life. Decluttering isn't just about getting rid of things—it's about creating space for what truly matters.

Adopt The "One-Year Rule"

A practical starting point in the decluttering process is the "one-year rule." If you never wore an item in the past year, you likely don't need it. This rule helps simplify decisions about what to keep and let go of. Apply this rule to everything in your closet, from clothes and shoes to accessories.

Creating Sorting Piles

As you examine each item, sort them into three piles: Keep, Donate, and Discard. Here's how to decide:

- **Keep**: Items that fit well are in good condition and match your lifestyle.
- **Donate**: Items in good condition that no longer fit your style or life.
- **Discard**: Worn out or damaged items that aren't suitable for donation.

Sorting into these piles will help you visually see how much you're choosing to hold onto versus what you're moving on from.

Tackling Decluttering In Stages

Starting with the most straightforward category, such as out-of-season clothes or items already in the discard pile, can make the process more manageable. You can maintain energy and motivation by breaking the task into manageable sections. Begin with items you feel less emotionally attached to and gradually work up to more challenging categories.

Mindful Decision Making

Adopting a thoughtful and critical approach to each item is essential as you begin sorting through your belongings. This process declutters your space and ensures that every item you keep has a purpose and adds value to your life. To facilitate this, consider the following questions for each piece:

1. **Does this item bring me joy?**

   Inspired by Marie Kondo, a well-known organizing consultant and author, this question is central to the KonMari method of tidying up. Kondo emphasizes the importance of keeping only those items that "spark joy." This emotional approach encourages you to surround yourself with things that uplift and enhance your life, making your space more harmonious and enjoyable.

2. **Is it functional in my current lifestyle?**

   Assessing the functionality of an item in your current lifestyle is crucial. It's important to consider whether a piece of clothing fits your daily activities or suits a life stage you've moved past. For example, work attire is essential in a corporate setting, but less so if you now work from home or have retired.

3. **Have I worn it in the last year?**

   This practical question helps you evaluate each item's actual use. If something has yet to be worn in a year, it's likely to continue to go unworn. This could be due to changes in taste, fit, or lifestyle. Identifying these pieces can significantly streamline your wardrobe, freeing up space and reducing clutter.

Being genuinely honest with your responses is critical to making effective decisions about what stays in your closet. This honesty will help you avoid holding onto items out of obligation, guilt, or inertia, which can all lead to a cluttered and disorganized space.

Through this critical evaluation, you align your wardrobe with your practical needs, joy, and lifestyle, creating a functional and delightfully curated closet. This method clears your physical space and supports a mindset of intentional living, where every item in your home contributes to your well-being and happiness.

Scheduling Decluttering Time

To ensure you follow through, schedule a specific time for decluttering in your calendar. Treat it like any other necessary appointment. Having a set time helps you commit to the task and prevents procrastination.

Decluttering your closet can be a liberating experience. It clears physical space, helps reduce stress, and improves mental clarity. By removing items you no longer use or need, you make room for things that serve a purpose in your life. Decluttering is not a one-time event but a continuous process that keeps your space functional and reflects your current needs.

CHAPTER 3: SORTING YOUR ITEMS

Organization is a journey, not a destination

— UNKNOWN

Now that you've decluttered your closet, it's time to sort the items you've decided to keep. This chapter will guide you through organizing these items effectively, ensuring that your closet looks appealing and functions efficiently. Sorting is about creating order and making your daily routine more manageable.

Sorting By Season And Function

Begin by grouping your clothes by season—winter, spring, summer, and autumn. This helps you quickly find what is appropriate for the weather and makes seasonal transitions smoother. Within each seasonal category, sort items by function: workwear, casual wear, formal attire, and activewear. This method lets you quickly locate the right outfit for any occasion without searching.

Using Bins And Labels For Temporary Categories

It can be helpful to temporarily use clear bins or labels to hold different categories during sorting. This not only aids in visual clarity but also decision-making, as you can move items around as you refine their placement. Labeling these bins or areas temporarily can also prevent mixing items up.

Involving A Second Opinion

Sometimes, involving a friend or family member in the sorting process is beneficial. They can offer a second opinion on what looks good and no longer fits your style or body. This is particularly useful for those items you're unsure about keeping.

Deciding On A Dedicated Spot For Each Category

Once you've established your categories, choose a

dedicated spot for each within your closet. Place the items you use most often in the most accessible spots. Rarely used items can go into the harder-to-reach areas. Think logically about placement: for example, keep all your work shirts together, so you don't have to search through casual t-shirts to find them on a busy morning.

Removing Items For Donation Or Disposal Immediately

To prevent second-guessing your decisions, immediately remove items designated for donation or disposal and arrange for them to be picked up or dropped off as soon as possible. This action prevents clutter from creeping back into your closet and helps maintain the clarity and openness you've worked hard to create.

Sorting your items efficiently after decluttering is crucial for maintaining a functional wardrobe. It ensures that everything in your closet has a purpose and a place, making your daily routine smoother and more enjoyable. Remember, the goal is not just to reduce the number of items but to organize them in a way that complements your lifestyle and preferences. By the end of this chapter, you should have a well-organized closet that makes getting dressed a simple and satisfying task.

STORAGE
SOLUTIONS

CHAPTER 4: UTILIZING CLOSET SPACE

If you want to improve your life immediately, clean out a closet. Often, it's what we hold onto that holds us back

— CHERYL RICHARDSON

Once you've completed the decluttering and sorting your items, the next phase involves maximizing every inch of your closet space. This approach not only helps to keep your closet organized but also ensures it can adapt to your evolving needs over time. You can transform an ordinary closet into a highly functional and efficient area by utilizing your available space.

Installing Adjustable Shelves

Adjustable shelving is a versatile tool in closet organization. It allows you to change the height of shelves based on what you need to store—whether it's tall boots, stacks of sweaters, or bins. With adjustable shelves, you can customize your storage space without permanent alterations, making it easy to adapt as your wardrobe changes.

Using The Back Of The Closet Door

The back of the closet door is often overlooked but offers valuable space for additional storage. Install hooks or over-the-door organizers for belts, hats, scarves, and bags. This frees up shelf and rod space and keeps these smaller items easily accessible and in good condition.

Opting For Multi-Level Hanging Rods

Multi-level hanging rods can dramatically increase the hanging space in your closet. You can hang shirts on one level and pants or skirts beneath them by installing two or more rods, one above the other. This setup is instrumental in closets with high ceilings and makes excellent use of vertical space.

Pull-Out Baskets For Frequent Use Items

Pull-out baskets can be a game-changer for items

you use frequently, such as workout clothes or undergarments. These baskets slide out for easy access and can be tucked away neatly when not in use. They help keep your most-used items at hand while keeping them organized and out of sight when necessary.

Top-Shelf Storage For Seldom-Used Items

Use the top shelf of your closet to store seldom-used items such as out-of-season clothing, travel bags, or extra bedding. Use clear storage bins with lids to keep these items clean and protected. Label each bin clearly to find what you need without unpacking everything.

Effectively utilizing the space in your closet can transform a cramped and cluttered area into a streamlined, functional wardrobe. By employing strategies such as adjustable shelves, door storage, multi-level rods, pull-out baskets, and top-shelf solutions, you can create a customized space that adapts to your lifestyle and makes getting ready each day a pleasure. Remember, the goal is to have a place for everything and everything in its place, saving you time and prolonging the life of your clothing by storing it properly.

CHAPTER 5: STORAGE ACCESSORIES

Your home is living space, not storage space

— FRANCINE JAY

In this chapter, we focus on maximizing your closet's efficiency and functionality through storage accessories. By incorporating intelligent storage solutions, you can organize your closet, make the most of every square inch, and ensure every item is easily accessible.

Slim, Non-Slip Hangers

One of the simplest yet most effective ways to improve your closet's capacity and keep it looking neat is by using slim, non-slip hangers.

These hangers take up less space than traditional ones, allowing you to fit more into your closet. Additionally, their non-slip surface prevents clothes from falling, keeping your garments securely in place.

Drawer Dividers For Small Items

Small items like socks, underwear, and accessories can easily become jumbled. Drawer dividers are excellent for keeping these items organized. They help you designate a specific spot for each type of item, making it easy to find what you need quickly without disrupting the order of your entire drawer.

Vertical Storage Options

Vertical storage solutions, such as hanging shelves or over-the-door organizers, are perfect for maximizing vertical space in your closet. These options are great for storing shoes, handbags, and other accessories, freeing up shelf and floor space for different uses.

Over-The-Door Organizers For Accessories

Over-the-door organizers are good for more than just shoes. They can be a great way to store various accessories, from jewelry and belts to scarves and hats. These organizers use unused space excellently and keep your accessories visible and accessible.

Over the door closet organizer

Under-Bed Storage For Off-Season Clothing

Consider using under-bed storage containers for off-season clothing to free up closet space. These containers keep your clothes dust-free and out of the way but still easily accessible when the seasons change. Opt for clear containers or those with a label window to quickly identify the contents without opening them.

Effective use of storage accessories can transform your closet from a chaotic space into a well-organized area that makes daily dressing a breeze. You can ensure every item has its place by choosing the right accessories, such as slim hangers, drawer dividers, vertical storage options, over-the-door organizers, and under-bed storage. This organization helps maintain the condition of your clothing and saves you time and stress, making your daily routine smoother and more enjoyable. With these tools, your closet will become a model of efficiency and order, supporting your lifestyle with simplicity and elegance.

CHAPTER 6: SEASONAL STORAGE TIPS

The first step in crafting the life you want is to get rid of everything you don't

— JOSHUA BECKER

As the seasons change, so do our wardrobe needs. This chapter offers practical advice for storing off-season clothing and accessories, ensuring they stay in excellent condition until you need them again. Practical seasonal storage frees up space in your closet for items you currently use and extends the life of your off-season garments by protecting them from damage and wear.

Selecting The Right Materials For Storage

Choosing suitable storage materials is crucial for protecting your clothing. For delicate items, breathable storage containers or bags are essential to prevent moisture buildup that can lead to mold or mildew. Avoid plastic bags, which can trap moisture; opt for fabric garment bags or natural fiber containers that allow air circulation.

Breathable Storage Containers

Breathable storage containers are your best bet for bulkier items like winter coats or heavy sweaters. These containers allow airflow, which is vital for keeping your clothes fresh. If space allows, place these containers under the bed or on top shelves in your closet. Make sure the containers are clean and dry before storing clothes in them.

Vacuum-Seal Bags For Bulky Items

Vacuum-seal bags are perfect for compressing bulky items like winter jackets, quilts, and fluffy sweaters. By removing the air, these bags significantly reduce the volume of these items, making them easier to store. However, using these bags judiciously is essential, as prolonged compression can damage certain fabrics. Use them for short-term storage and check the items periodically.

Rotating Closet Items By Season

To keep your closet functional and manageable, rotate your clothing by season. As one season ends, clean and store those items away, bringing forward the clothes for the upcoming season. This rotation not only optimizes your closet space but also gives you a chance to review each item's condition and fit before it goes into or comes out of storage.

Cleaning Items Before Storage

Always clean your clothes before storing them for the season. Dirt and oils can set into fabrics over time and make them harder to clean, which can attract pests. Make sure every item is dry before storage to prevent mold growth. This cleaning rule also applies to shoes, boots, and outerwear.

Tips For Using Space-Saving Solutions

Maximize your storage space with these tips:

- Use clear bins to quickly identify contents without needing to open each container.
- Label each bin with a description of its contents and the date stored.
- Store heavier items at the bottom and lighter ones on top to prevent crushing.

- Keep a detailed inventory list of stored items to avoid unnecessary purchases or duplicates.

Seasonal storage is a critical aspect of closet management that helps you maintain a clutter-free environment and preserve the quality of your clothing. By using appropriate materials, cleaning items before storage, and rotating your wardrobe seasonally, you can ensure that your clothes remain in excellent condition year after year. These storage tips will save time and money, making seasonal transitions smooth and stress-free.

MAINTENANCE STRATEGIES

CHAPTER 7:
DAILY HABITS

For every minute spent organizing, an hour is earned

— BENJAMIN FRANKLIN

Maintaining an organized closet isn't just about the initial setup—it requires ongoing attention. This chapter focuses on establishing habits that help keep your closet in order. By integrating simple, consistent practices into your routine, you can ensure that your closet remains a functional and pleasant space.

Putting Clothes Away Immediately

A fundamental habit that can dramatically improve the state of your closet is putting clothes away immediately after use or laundry. Resist the urge to throw clothes on a chair or the floor. By hanging up or folding clothes right away, you prevent the buildup of clutter and reduce your workload later.

Maintaining A Donation Box

Keep a donation bag or box in your closet. Whenever you try on something that no longer fits or isn't to your taste anymore, put it straight into the donation box. This habit helps you continuously curate your wardrobe and prevents items that you don't wear from taking up valuable space.

Setting Weekly Quick Tidy-Ups

Choose a specific day and time each week for a quick closet sweep. This 10 to 15-minute routine should involve rehanging fallen clothes, refolding messy stacks, and putting away any items that ended up in your closet but don't belong there. This regular maintenance prevents small messes from turning into big ones.

Outfit Planning The Night Before

To minimize mess and stress, get into the habit of planning your outfits the night before. This saves you time in the morning and keeps your closet tidy because you won't be rummaging through it in a rush. You can use a valet hook or a dedicated area to lay out or hang the next day's clothing.

Implementing The 'One In, One Out' Rule

To maintain the balance in your closet, adopt the 'one in, one out' rule: for every new item that enters your closet, one should leave. This practice keeps your wardrobe manageable and ensures you genuinely need and love each piece you purchase.

Incorporating these daily habits into your routine can transform how you manage your closet. Each habit prevents clutter and maintains organization, ultimately making your closet a space of ease and efficiency. Over time, these practices will become second nature, and you'll enjoy the benefits of a well-maintained wardrobe daily.

CHAPTER 8: WEEKLY ROUTINES

When you organize your life around what you love, everything finds its place

— UNKNOWN

It's essential to establish regular weekly routines to keep your closet in optimal shape. This chapter outlines a series of weekly practices designed to maintain the organization and longevity of your wardrobe, ensuring your closet remains a functional and orderly space.

Designate A Day For Closet Maintenance

Choose one day each week, perhaps a Sunday afternoon or a weekday evening, to dedicate to closet upkeep. This routine doesn't have to be lengthy—a focused 20 to 30-minute session can suffice. The key is consistency; sticking to a schedule will help make these tasks habitual and less daunting.

Quick Closet Sweep

Begin your weekly routine with a quick closet sweep. This includes rehanging any clothes that may have slipped off hangers, refolding items that have been disrupted, and checking for items that need to be laundered. A neat closet is easier to navigate and keeps your clothes in better condition.

Inspect Clothes For Repairs

As you tidy, inspect your garments for any needed repairs. Look for missing buttons, loose threads, or minor tears. Set aside any items that need mending. Addressing these issues promptly prevents minor damages from becoming significant problems, extending the life of your clothing.

Update Your Organization System

Your lifestyle and needs may evolve, so it's beneficial to reassess your closet organization periodically. As you go through your weekly routine, consider whether the current system still works for you. Maybe your work attire needs to be more accessible, or seasonal items are no longer in the right place. Adjust as needed.

Monthly Mini-Declutter Sessions

Incorporate a mini-declutter session into your routine monthly as part of your weekly activity. This doesn't need to be as intensive as your seasonal decluttering—simply scan your wardrobe for any items that no longer fit, that you haven't worn in a while, or that don't meet your current needs. This regular pruning keeps your closet relevant and manageable.

Natural Fresheners To Keep Your Closet Smelling Clean

To ensure your closet looks clean and smells fresh, consider using natural fresheners. Lavender sachets, cedar blocks, or a small container of baking soda can absorb odors and add a pleasant scent to your space. Refresh these as needed during your weekly routines.

Implementing these weekly routines will help maintain the functionality and appearance of your closet over time. By dedicating just a tiny fraction of your week to these practices, you can enjoy a well-organized and pleasant wardrobe that makes getting ready each day simpler and more enjoyable. Regular maintenance helps you stay organized and fosters a sense of calm and preparedness, making your daily routine more efficient.

CHAPTER 9:
THE MONTHLY
OVERHAUL

*You will never get organized if you don't have a
vision for your life*

— LINDA L. EUBANKS

While daily and weekly habits are crucial for
maintaining an orderly closet, a more thorough
monthly overhaul can ensure deeper care and
organization. This chapter guides you through
conducting a monthly review and cleanup of your
closet, ensuring every aspect remains in top shape
and effectively serves your current needs.

Plan A Thorough Cleaning

Begin your monthly overhaul by scheduling a

day for deep cleaning. This includes dusting all surfaces, vacuuming the closet floor, and wiping down shelves and drawers. Remove all items from the closet to reach every nook and cranny. A clean environment will protect your clothes from dust and pests and make your closet a more pleasant place to access daily.

Reassess Your Organizational System

Each month, take the time to reassess the effectiveness of your organizational system. Your needs might shift as seasons change or as new items are added. Ask yourself:

- Are the most frequently used items easily accessible?
- Do seasonal items need to be rotated?
- Could the space be optimized better?

Make adjustments as necessary to ensure the layout of your closet matches your current lifestyle and clothing use.

Rotate Seasonal Items

Particularly in months transitioning between seasons, take the opportunity to rotate out clothes that will no longer be used. For example, at the end of winter, pack away heavy sweaters and coats and bring forward spring garments. This frees up space and makes it easier to find appropriate clothing for the current weather.

Review Wear And Usage

During your monthly overhaul, review what items have been worn and what haven't. This can provide valuable insights into which clothes are genuinely beneficial in your wardrobe and which may be candidates for donation or sale. Consider the "one-year rule" — if it hasn't been worn in the last year, it might be time to let it go.

Check For Needed Repairs And Cleaning

As you handle each piece, check for any needed repairs or cleaning. Identify clothes that require special attention, such as professional dry cleaning or tailoring. Addressing these issues promptly will keep your wardrobe in ready-to-wear condition and extend the life of your garments.

Reflect On Your Organization Goals

End your monthly overhaul by reflecting on your organizational goals:

- Have you achieved the level of order you desire?
- Are there areas that consistently need to be more organized?

- What new strategies could you implement?

This reflection will help you continuously improve the functionality and enjoyment of your closet space.

A monthly closet overhaul is an excellent practice that complements your daily and weekly habits. It allows for a deeper inspection and maintenance of your wardrobe, ensuring that your organization stays relevant and practical. By dedicating time to clean, reassess, and adjust your closet regularly, you maintain not just a well-organized space but also a wardrobe that genuinely suits your current life. This process helps make your daily routine smoother and keeps your attire in its best condition, ready for any occasion.

ADVANCED ORGANIZATION TECHNIQUES

CHAPTER 10:
COLOR CODING

Clutter is nothing more than postponed decisions

— BARBARA HEMPHILL

Color coding your closet is not just about creating a visually appealing space; it's a practical approach that streamlines your process of selecting outfits. This chapter will guide you on organizing your wardrobe by color, which can speed up your daily routine and make maintaining your closet easier.

Benefits Of Organizing Clothes By Color

Color coding helps you quickly locate items, saving time during your daily outfit selection. It also makes it easier to see what colors you wear most and which colors you need more to balance your wardrobe. Additionally, a color-coordinated closet reduces the time spent on reorganizing, as items naturally find their place back more intuitively.

Starting With Light Colors And Moving To Darker Shades

Begin by grouping your clothes from light to dark. This usually starts with whites and pastels, moving through to yellows, pinks, greens, blues, browns, grays, and ending with black. This spectrum creates an aesthetically pleasing gradient and mirrors the way colors are often found in retail stores, making it easier for you to conceptualize your wardrobe.

Grouping Prints And Patterns Separately

After sorting solid colors, tackle your prints and patterns. Because these items are more visually distinctive, they're easier to spot when stored together. Grouping all patterned clothing in one section of your closet, regardless of color, helps keep the focus on solid colors while making these more decorative pieces easy to access.

Using Color-Coded Hangers Or Tags

To enhance your color-coding system, consider using color-coded hangers or tags. For instance, use pink hangers for red items, blue for denim, etc. This method reinforces the visual organization of your closet and can be particularly helpful if you have many clothes or share a wardrobe with someone else.

How Color Coding Can Speed Up Your Daily Routine

Color coding is more than just pleasing to the eye; it optimizes your decision-making process. With a well-organized color-coded closet, you can quickly bypass colors that don't match the occasion or your mood, heading straight to the section that meets your needs. This system saves precious minutes each morning, adding up to hours over a month.

Closet with clothes organized by color

Implementing a color-coding system in your closet offers numerous benefits beyond simple aesthetics. It transforms your closet into an efficient, easy-to-navigate space, reduces the time and effort needed to pick out outfits, and can even make putting laundry away simpler and faster. Following the steps outlined in this chapter, you can enjoy a beautifully organized wardrobe that complements your lifestyle and enhances your daily routine.

CHAPTER 11: ACCESSORY FOCUS

Have nothing in your house that you do not know to be useful, or believe to be beautiful

— WILLIAM MORRIS

Accessories are often the finishing touches that complete an outfit, but they can quickly become cluttered if improperly organized. This chapter focuses on efficient and effective ways to organize and store accessories such as ties, scarves, belts, jewelry, and more, ensuring they remain in good condition and are easy to find.

Using Specialized Hangers For Ties, Scarves, And Belts

Use specialized hangers to keep ties, scarves, and belts organized and prevent them from becoming wrinkled or damaged. These hangers are designed to hold multiple items at once, making them easily accessible while saving space. They also allow you to see all your options at a glance, making selecting the right accessory for your outfit easier.

Drawer Organizers For Smaller Accessories

Smaller accessories like jewelry can quickly become tangled or lost. Drawer organizers are an excellent solution for keeping these items sorted and protected. Choose organizers with compartments of various sizes to accommodate multiple items such as earrings, rings, watches, and bracelets. This organization helps prevent damage and makes finding what you're looking for easier without rummaging.

Wall-Mounted Racks For Hats And Bags

Consider using wall-mounted racks to save shelf space and keep hats and bags in shape. These racks provide a dedicated spot for each item, which helps maintain their form and makes them easy to grab on the go. Placing these racks at an appropriate height can also enhance the decor of your room while keeping your accessories organized.

Wall mounted rack for hats and bags

Care And Storage Of Luxury Accessories

Luxury accessories require special care to maintain their condition. Store such items in custom-fitted cases or original packaging to protect them from dust, light, and moisture. For high-end items like designer bags and shoes, consider investing in products like silica gel packs to control humidity in storage areas, preserving the quality and extending the lifespan of these valuable pieces.

Introducing Modular Storage Systems

MModular storage systems can be adapted for a flexible storage solution for a flexible storage solution to fit various types of accessories. These systems allow you to add, remove, or rearrange components such as shelves, drawers, and hooks to accommodate your changing collection. Modular systems are handy because they can be customized to the specific sizes and shapes of items you own.

Organizing your accessories makes your daily routine more efficient and helps you enjoy and use your items more effectively. By implementing the right storage solutions—specialized hangers, drawer organizers, wall-mounted racks, and modular systems—you ensure that your accessories are preserved in good condition and are always ready to enhance your outfits. Proper accessory organization not only saves you time but also adds a level of enjoyment to dressing up by easily showcasing your options.

CHAPTER 12: TECH TOOLS TO HELP

Outer order contributes to inner calm

— GRETCHEN RUBIN

In today's digital age, technology offers innovative solutions to enhance closet organization. This chapter explores various tech tools that can help you manage your wardrobe more efficiently. From apps that assist in tracking and planning outfits to gadgets that streamline the maintenance of your clothes, technology can transform the way you interact with your closet.

Wardrobe And Outfit Planning Apps

Several smartphone apps allow you to catalog your

clothes and plan outfits. These apps often feature tools for taking photos of your items, tagging them by category, and creating a calendar for what to wear and when. Apps like Stylebook and Cladwell help you visualize different combinations and suggest outfits based on the weather or occasion, making daily dressing decisions more straightforward and quicker.

Online Resources For Diy Closet Organization

For those who prefer a hands-on approach to organization, numerous online platforms offer DIY tips and tutorials for custom closet solutions. Websites like Pinterest and YouTube are full of creative ideas and step-by-step guides, from building a closet system to making your own accessory holders. These resources can be beneficial if you want to customize your space without spending a fortune.

Inventory Management Apps

Inventory management apps can be invaluable for individuals with extensive wardrobes or those managing family clothing. These apps allow you to keep a detailed record of your wardrobe, including where items are stored, their size, condition and even cost. This can be extremely helpful for insurance purposes, planning seasonal rotations, or simply keeping track of what you have to avoid unnecessary purchases.

Virtual Closets For Visualizing Outfits

Some advanced apps offer a feature known as a "virtual closet," which allows you to see your clothes in a digital format. This can be particularly useful for mixing and matching pieces to see how they look together before physically trying them on. Virtual closets can save you time and help you utilize your wardrobe to its full potential by pairing items you might have yet to think to combine.

Home Automation Tools For Closet Management

For a high-tech closet experience, consider integrating home automation tools. Bright lighting can be installed to enhance visibility or highlight specific closet areas. Automated hanging systems or motorized shelves can make accessing items easier, especially in large or tall closets. These systems can be controlled via smartphone, making them functional and a fun addition to your home.

Incorporating technology into your closet organization can significantly enhance the functionality and enjoyment of your wardrobe management. Whether through apps that simplify outfit planning and inventory tracking or DIY resources that inspire creative storage solutions, technology offers tools that cater to every organizational need and preference. By embracing these tech tools, you can streamline your daily routines, make informed decisions about your clothing, and enjoy a closet that is as modern as it is organized.

BONUS SECTION - ORGANIZING YOUR BATHROOM

CHAPTER 13: DECLUTTERING YOUR BATHROOM

Tidying is just a tool, not the final destination

— MARIE KONDO

Just like your closet, your bathroom can benefit significantly from regular decluttering and organization. This chapter focuses on strategies to streamline your bathroom space, enhancing its functionality and aesthetics. Decluttering your bathroom creates a more calming environment and improves hygiene and usability.

Clean and decluttered bathroom

Applying Decluttering Principles To The Bathroom

Start by applying a similar decluttering process to your bathroom as you would to your closet. Begin by removing all items from bathroom shelves, drawers, and cabinets. This will give you a clear view of what you have, what you use, and what can be discarded or stored elsewhere.

Focus On Expiration Dates

Pay special attention to expiration dates on cosmetics and medicines. Expired products can be ineffective or harmful, so it's essential to check and dispose of outdated items routinely. This frees up space and ensures that everything in your bathroom is safe to use.

Organize Items By Frequency Of Use

Organize your bathroom items based on how frequently you use them. Everyday items like toothpaste, daily skincare products, and your favorite shampoos should be easily accessible, possibly at eye level or in an open area. Less frequently used items, such as unique occasion makeup or spare toiletries, can be stored higher up or in deeper storage.

Maintaining A Minimalist Counter

Aim for a minimalist approach to counter space to keep your bathroom looking neat and to make cleaning easier. Store only essential items on the countertop, and use organizational trays or holders to keep these items tidy. This not only helps keep your bathroom clean but also makes it visually appealing.

Encourage Regular Updates

As products are used up or replaced, take the

opportunity to reevaluate what's stored in your bathroom. This regular updating prevents the accumulation of unused or unnecessary items and helps maintain an organized space. It also allows you to adapt your storage solutions to changing needs and preferences.

Decluttering your bathroom is critical to maintaining a functional and relaxing home environment. By regularly assessing and organizing the contents of your bathroom, focusing on the usability of items, and maintaining a minimalist approach to storage, you can ensure your bathroom remains a tidy and welcoming space. Implementing these strategies will enhance your bathroom's appearance and functionality, making your daily routines smoother and more enjoyable.

CHAPTER 14: STORAGE SOLUTIONS FOR BATHROOMS

Happiness is a place between too little and too much

— FINNISH PROVERB

Practical storage solutions are crucial for maintaining an organized and functional bathroom, especially in homes with limited space. This chapter explores ways to maximize storage efficiency in your bathroom, keeping essential items accessible while maintaining a clutter-free environment.

Under-Sink Storage Solutions

In many bathrooms, the area under the sink should be more utilized. Organizers and storage bins can significantly increase storage capacity. Consider installing pull-out drawers or shelves, which will make accessing items more manageable and organized. Bins and baskets can also be used to separate products and keep like items together, such as cleaning supplies, hair care products, and skincare items.

Under sink storage solutions

Over-The-Toilet Shelving

The space above the toilet can be ideal for additional

shelving. Installing shelves or cabinets above the toilet can provide a convenient place to store towels, toiletries, and other bathroom essentials. This helps in utilizing vertical space and keeps daily necessities within reach without cluttering the counter.

Drawer Dividers For Makeup And Small Toiletries

Drawer dividers can be a game-changer for smaller items such as makeup, razors, or dental care products. These dividers help compartmentalize your drawers, making it easy to find what you need and preventing items from being jumbled together. This organization can save time during your daily routine and avoid the frustration of searching through disorganized drawers.

Vertical Storage Options

Vertical space is often available in bathrooms but needs to be adequately utilized. Installing tall, narrow cabinets or open shelving can provide significant additional storage without taking up much floor space. These can be used for storing extra towels, bath products, and other toiletries. Additionally, vertical storage can help draw the eye upward, making the bathroom appear larger.

Water-Resistant Materials For Storage

Choosing water-resistant materials for your storage solutions is essential for a bathroom's moist environment. Materials such as plastic, stainless steel, or treated wood can withstand humidity and frequent exposure to water, ensuring longevity and maintaining the appearance of your storage units.

Recommendations For Towels And Washcloths

Open shelving or baskets can offer a convenient and visually appealing storage solution for towels and washcloths. Rolling towels instead of folding them can save space and create an inviting display. For practical usability, ensure that these storage solutions are within easy reach of the shower or bath.

Implementing effective storage solutions in your bathroom can transform a typically cluttered area into a well-organized and functional space. By utilizing under-sink areas, over-the-toilet spaces, drawer dividers, and vertical storage, you can significantly increase the storage capacity of your bathroom. Choosing appropriate materials and organizing items efficiently enhances the bathroom's functionality and contributes to a cleaner, more streamlined appearance. These improvements can make daily routines more pleasant and efficient, allowing for a stress-free start and end to your day.

CHAPTER 15: MAINTAINING ORDER IN YOUR BATHROOM

The best way to find out what we need is to get rid of what we don't

— MARIE KONDO

Keeping your bathroom organized is not just about creating a system but maintaining it. Regular upkeep ensures that your bathroom remains a functional and calming space. This chapter provides practical strategies for sustaining order and cleanliness in your bathroom, helping you to extend the fresh and organized feeling long after you've set up your space.

Daily Surface Wiping

Incorporate daily surface wiping into your routine. After using the sink and countertop, take a minute to wipe down the surfaces with a microfiber cloth or disposable wipe. This habit prevents the buildup of toothpaste splatters, makeup stains, and water spots, which can make your bathroom look untidy. Maintaining clean surfaces daily makes deeper, weekly cleanings much more manageable.

Weekly Review Of Item Placement

Once a week, quickly review to ensure all items are in their designated spots. This check includes putting away any items that were used and not returned to their place, like toiletries, towels, and small appliances. Regular checks help prevent clutter from accumulating and make cleaning and use of your bathroom space easier.

Seasonal Checks For Expirations And Updates

Conduct a more thorough check every few months to sort through products, especially cosmetics and medications. Check expiration dates and remove items that are outdated or no longer used. This not only helps maintain health and safety but also frees up space for products that are in use.

Implement Good Ventilation Practices

Proper ventilation is crucial in a bathroom to prevent mold and mildew, which can damage surfaces and create unhealthy air. Always use an exhaust fan during and after showers or baths, and consider leaving it on for about 30 minutes afterward. If your bathroom lacks a fan, habitually open a window to air out the space regularly.

Encourage Consistent Habits

The key to maintaining order in your bathroom, as in any part of your home, is consistency. Encourage all household members to adopt habits that support cleanliness and organization. This might include hanging up towels, replacing toiletries after use, and keeping personal items stored away rather than on counters.

Practical Accessory Usage

Make practical use of accessories to help maintain order. For instance, a toothbrush holder prevents brushes from lying on surfaces, and a soap dish or dispenser keeps soap contained and tidy. These small organizers contribute significantly to keeping the area clean and orderly.

Maintaining an organized bathroom requires regular attention but doesn't need to be time-consuming. By integrating these simple habits into your daily and weekly routines, you can keep your bathroom looking and feeling clean and organized for longer. This proactive approach makes your bathroom more enjoyable and simplifies cleaning and upkeep, enhancing your overall quality of life at home.

CONCLUSION: BRINGING IT ALL TOGETHER

Organizing is not about perfection; it's about efficiency, reducing stress and clutter, saving time and money, and improving your overall quality of life

— CHRISTINA SCALISE

Reflecting on the transformation is essential as we conclude our journey through organizing closets and bathrooms. The structured approaches and techniques discussed in previous chapters aren't merely about tidying up—they're about cultivating a mindset that values efficiency, tranquility, and clarity in every aspect of home life. An organized space leads to a more organized mind, enabling better focus, reduced stress, and improved quality of life.

The Benefits Revisited

Throughout this guide, we explored various benefits of organization:

- **Psychological Clarity:** A clutter-free environment reduces anxiety and enhances mental clarity. Simple daily routines and well-maintained spaces support a healthier, more focused mindset.
- **Time Savings:** By implementing systems for routine maintenance, we save precious time daily. These efficiencies accumulate, giving us more moments for relaxation and quality time with loved ones.
- **Economic Advantages:** Maintaining an organized space helps you manage belongings more effectively, avoid unnecessary purchases, and ultimately save money.
- **Aesthetic Enjoyment:** Beyond functionality, an organized space is visually pleasing. The simplicity and order create a serene home environment that welcomes relaxation and contentment.

Future Steps For Continuous Improvement

Organization is an ongoing process. As life changes,

your organizational needs will also evolve. Here are a few tips for adapting the strategies you've learned:

- **Continuous Learning:** Keep seeking new ideas and innovations in home organization. The organization world constantly evolves, and staying informed can provide new tools and methods to enhance your space.
- **Feedback and Adaptation:** Listen to feedback from family members about the organizational systems in place. Their insights can help refine your approaches, ensuring the systems benefit everyone.
- **Experimentation:** Don't be afraid to change and experiment with different configurations and techniques. What works today may not be as effective tomorrow, so stay flexible and open to adjustments.

Expand Organizational Practices

Now that you've experienced the benefits of organizing your closet and bathroom consider applying these principles to other areas of your home, like your kitchen, living room, or home office. Each space has unique challenges and opportunities for improving functionality and aesthetics.

Final Thoughts

Remember, organization is not about perfection. It's about creating spaces that support your lifestyle and make daily routines more manageable. Each small step towards organizing your home contributes to a more significant impact on your overall well-being and happiness. Keep moving forward, keep adjusting, and enjoy the benefits of a beautifully organized home.

As a small independent publisher, I would love to hear your thoughts. Please leave a review on Amazon. Simply click THIS LINK

Thanks for reading!

PS - If you'd like a free copy of my book on how to clean anything and keep it that way in less than 15 minutes a day, visit KevinWagonfoot.com

Made in the USA
Columbia, SC
02 July 2025

60221627R00046